ONE DAY I STARTED A NEW LiFE

ONE DAY I STARTED A NEW LIFE

STACY RUSSO

Litwin Books ★ 2024

Copyright 2024 Stacy Russo.

Published in 2024 by Litwin Books.

Litwin Books, LLC
PO Box 188784
Sacramento, CA 95818

http://litwinbooks.com/

This book is printed on acid-free paper.

Cover and book design by Josh MacPhee.
This book is set in Libertario and Avenir Next.

Publisher's Cataloging in Publication

Names: Russo, Stacy Shotsberger.
Title: One day I started a new life / Stacy Russo.
Description: Sacramento, CA : Litwin Books, 2024.
Identifiers: LCCN 2024935473 | ISBN 9781634001557 (acid-free paper)
Subjects: LCSH: Russo, Stacy Shotsberger – Biography. | Librarians as artists.
| Librarians' writings.
| Artists – United States – Biography. | Librarians – United States – Biography.
Classification: LCC N7433.4.A2 R87 2024 | DDC 700.92 R--dc23
LC record available at https://lccn.loc.gov/2024935473

Previous page spread:
Imagininary Map Library, 12 x 9, watercolor paint, acrylic paint, watercolor pencils, magazine paper, newspaper, and map paper on mixed media paper, 2019

Opposite:
California Dreaming (My Mom and Grandma in California), 19 x 12.5, watercolor paint, watercolor pencils, acrylic paint, magazine paper, and lokta paper on art paper, 2023

Also by Stacy Russo

NONFICTION
The Library as Place in California
Love Activism
We Were Going to Change the World: Interviews with Women from the 1970s and 1980s Southern California Punk Rock Scene
A Better World Starts Here: Activists and Their Work
BEYOND 70: The Lives of Creative Women

FICTION
Stella Peabody's Wild Librarian Bakery and Bookstore

EDITED COLLECTIONS
Life as Activism: June Jordan's Writings from The Progressive
Feminist Pilgrimage: Journeys of Discovery
Wild Crone Wisdom: Poetry and Stories (with Julie Artman)

POETRY
Everyday Magic
The Moon and Other Poems

CHILDREN'S BOOKS
Poetry Hounds
Wild Librarian Bakery and Bookstore

*for my family -
my mom, dad, and brother*

Talking with My Spirit Family, 9 x 12, watercolor paint, watercolor pencils, pen, and magazine paper on mixed media paper, 2021

CONTENTS

Introduction: My Creative Journey	1
Collage and Mixed Media	18
Mixed Media Memoir	86
Children's Book Illustration	116

INTRODUCTION: MY CREATIVE JOURNEY

It's true that *One Day I Started a New Life*. I will tell you about this day and the new life that followed, which is when my creativity, courage, and life as an artist bloomed, but first there are earlier parts of my story I'd like to share.

My Dad's Magnificent Garden

When I was working on my book *BEYOND 70: The Lives of Creative Women* (Nauset Press), I interviewed twenty-one inspirational women between the ages of 70 and 98 about their lives. One woman I interviewed is a writer, one is primarily a musician, and the others are visual artists. I asked each woman a version of the question, "How did you become an artist?" This question was answered in twenty-one unique and compelling ways. If someone asked me this question, I would probably begin by describing my dad's garden.

My Mom and Dad in the 1950s

I was born in Harrisburg, Pennsylvania, in 1970. My family lived outside of the city in the small town of Mechanicsburg. We were a family of four (my parents, my older brother, David, and I) who lived in a small house full of love. By the time I was born, my parents had climbed their way to the middle class, but there was always worry about money and a feeling that we were just hanging on to the lower rungs of a ladder. My dad worked as a manager at a large warehouse. My mom worked as a janitor when I was little, and later in clerical jobs. Things my brother desired, musical instruments and motorcycles, were out of reach, but my main longing was books, which was easily satisfied at the public library and school book fairs.

Many things from that time are vivid in my memory with the most significant being the large backyard where my dad tended a magnificent food garden. Copies of *Organic Gardening* were scattered throughout the house and near his reading chair in the living room. When I try to list the fruits and vegetables that he seemed to effortlessly grow and harvest, I'm certain I'm forgetting some. I remember peaches, apples, blueberries, strawberries, cherries, honeydew melons, watermelon, cucumbers, green beans, cantaloupe, squash, zucchini, lettuce, Brussels sprouts, corn, and varieties of potatoes and tomatoes. In the center of all of this, near the middle of the yard and to the side of the strawberry patch, was an area with several tall trees. On the shady ground there, a lush bed of violets would appear when the weather was warm.

The landscape of my childhood has my dad's garden at the center. It was not only beautiful to walk and play there with my dog, a Border Collie mix from the Humane Society named Smokey, taking in the varied scents and colors, but it was also a place where my imagination ran wild. Only out in the garden would my imaginary friend named Priscilla appear. She was so well-known that our neighbors, seeing me talking outside by myself, would ask me how Priscilla was doing.

I credit my dad's garden as the beginning of my creative life. I saw the cycles of life there, got nourishment from what was grown, played within an ever-changing rainbow of colors, and spent the summers and weekends making up stories and poems. It is no surprise that my dad's garden sometimes appears in my visual art.

California, Punk Rock, and Zines

In 1981, when I was age eleven and about to enter my last year of elementary school, my dad was offered a warehouse manager job in the Los Angeles County city of Maywood. I believe his company was closing the Pennsylvania location, but I can't recall the particulars of the situation.

Me in 1986

California seemed as foreign as another country to us. The only member of my family that I remember ever traveling to California was my feisty and independent maternal grandmother, Evelyn Grace. Many years before my birth, she took a solo train journey across the country. I don't recall the existence of any photographs from this trip, but I remember hearing about her discovery of a delicious thing called an avocado. This story about avocados was passed down to my brother and I, which made California seem like a magical and mysterious place. When my parents shared the news that we were moving to California, I could not believe that I would soon be so lucky to live alongside movie stars and famous musicians. We imagined California as that: a place full of celebrities and sunshine where we could go to the ocean every day if we wanted and eat food that couldn't be bought in Pennsylvania grocery stores.

Now that I am in my middle years, my parents' decision to move their entire lives to an unknown place 3,000 miles away has become more meaningful to me. This move was mired in uncertainty and risk. It required selling our small home, letting go of the garden (my dad would never have a garden again), and relocating to rental properties, including different condominiums and apartments over the years, with an awareness that having the stability that home ownership had provided was likely no longer within our economic means. The move was also fueled by my parents' difficult experiences of growing up poor, which caused them to fear that financial ruin was always lurking in the shadows. Having a job was the most important thing. Still, even if fear of unemployment was a main ingredient for the move, there was also a good amount of faith, courage, resilience, wonder, and adventure. I wish I could ask them now about the move to understand more about the decision.

Moving to California forever changed my family's story. It was a great decision because the world became larger and full of possibilities. My brother, already an adult, got a motorcycle that he rode all around the canyons and desert. My dad thought the freeways were wonderful. He was also swept away by Hollywood. We were always driving to different studios to watch television shows being taped. The people we lived amongst were fascinating and eccentric, including a blond woman who sometimes walked around the complex sipping wine and wearing sheets for dresses and a strange middle-aged man who played with various tiny remote control cars and planes in the alley. We also thought illegal things with stolen cars were happening in a garage we could see from a window in my parent's bedroom. There was nothing this exciting in Mechanicsburg. My dad grew several robust tomato plants in a small patch of dirt and cared for a few potted plants, which seemed to somehow satisfy his gardening soul. For all we gave up, California gave back much more. I remember my dad once proclaiming, "Can you believe that we can get in the car and within five minutes there are so many good places to eat?!" Another Dad comment from our early days in California was, "This place is great! The smog must have killed all the bugs."

My parents had me late when they were in their forties. They were already in their fifties when we moved, demonstrating to my brother and I that one could start a new life at any age. This is one of the greatest gifts my parents gave us. Two things, California and the ability to start over, have always been linked together in my mind.

Within a few years of moving to California, I was completely immersed in the punk rock scene. It was the 1980s, which was a vibrant time for music. I suppose like many young girls with a rebellious streak, there were a few years where all I mostly cared about was boys, music, and partying. Most weekends I was out at the clubs: the Whisky, Roxy, Hollywood Palladium, Fender's Ballroom, and countless random dumps. Two lines from Social Distortion's song "Story of My Life," perfectly sums up how I felt back then: "I didn't have much interest in sports or school elections / And in class I dreamed all day 'bout a rock 'n' roll weekend." It wasn't only about drinking, music, and looking for boys though, growing up in the scene is the most influential element of my creativity and belief system. I was politicized through punk rock. I became aware of and outraged by the various forms of oppression tied to race, class, and gender. I went to political protests, discovered feminism, saw the trappings of materialism and consumer culture, and realized a lot of what I had been taught in school was often not true and sometimes outright racist. I discovered animal rights, becoming vegetarian in 1986 and later vegan, something I hold dear that brings me daily joy. I also discovered a DIY (do-it-yourself) ethic and a celebration of experimentation, which is probably the key element that has made me move forward with my art and writing.

At the kitchen counter where I make most of my art

Through punk rock, I saw that you didn't need to wait for a publisher or a record company to tell you that you were talented enough to be a writer or an artist. You also didn't need to wait until you got "good" or "perfect." Hell, you didn't even need to study stuff unless you wanted to. All you needed was some desire, imagination, and grit. In the 1980s, along with a group of friends, I created fanzines, which are self-published magazines, booklets, or pamphlets. The main fanzine we created was a political zine titled *Anti-Establishment*. We were teenage DIY journalists. I was amazed that I could write something and just put it out there in the world. The power of that for a young person is huge. Creating zines was also my first taste of collage, since the fanzine was entirely a cut-and-paste creation with text and images floating together in a chaotic, but still readable, format. In my late teens and twenties, I moved on from *Anti-Establishment* and other political punk creations to make zines showcasing my poetry. I also started to make collages on large pieces of cardboard. I mostly used recycled magazines or other "trash" items. Writing directly on the collage or composing text with letters from magazine headlines was often part of my early artmaking.

During the making of collages in my later teenage years and early twenties, I also began to discover something quite amazing. I realized that creating a collage would take away or minimize sadness, heartbreak, worry, and depression. Although I never articulated it back then, like many people I gravitated toward artmaking as a means of self-care and self-therapy. I certainly did not think of myself as an artist and had no plans to study art, but some of these large collages were so meaningful to me that I took them with me when I went away to college. I remember hanging them with tacks on the walls of the small room my parents helped me rent in Berkeley. One day several years ago I came across an old photo of me sitting in my Berkeley room. Behind me on the wall I could see a few inches of one of those beloved collages that I no longer have. When I saw it, my heart leapt, like if you unexpectedly notice someone you loved from long ago in the background of a photo.

UC Berkeley and June Jordan

As a teenager and then after high school I started working in various "hell jobs." I thought that was simply what one did as an adult – endure work and look forward to the evenings and weekends. I worked as a Ross Dress-for-Less fitting room clerk; in an awful job at a florist where I dipped my hands into ice cold water while using a metal device to remove thorns on roses (my hands would ache after and it took awhile for me to warm my body up); on the graveyard shift at a crappy motel by the freeway where the manager showed me a bat behind the counter on my first day and told me to use it if anyone tried to rob the place; and as a receptionist at a printing company where I experienced sexual harassment each day, including being asked about my breasts and bra size and enduring the men's stories about their sexual adventures and lunch time visits to a strip club. Some things were cruel and pure objectification.

On occasion at the receptionist job, I had to walk through the plant to my boss' office. Once, as I made my way by the large printing press of the men's domain where no women worked, the catcalls started and one of the men slapped me on my butt which caused a loud uproar of applause and cheering. I remember one man caught my eye and looked kindly at me with compassion, but sticking up for me would have been too much for him to risk in that toxic environment. It was painful to discover that how I could contribute with my mind or creativity was of no value. Some nights I would cry, wondering if this is what it was just going to be like as a woman in the world. My independence and fiery punk rock spirit was still with me, but the working world was a grind. When I fought back and tried to stick up for myself it only made the guys more excited. I told them off and they laughed, cheered, and made obscene gestures. I now understand they were able to be bold and act in these ways because they knew they had the power and would not face any repercussions. I lasted eight months in that job before I quit.

During this time, I continued to write, make collages, and go out often to see live music, but I didn't have much guidance on possibilities for making a creative life or finding a fulfilling career where I may be valued. This is no fault of my beautiful parents, since they did not go to college and believed finishing high school and getting a job were major accomplishments. Securing a full-time receptionist or secretary job right out of high school was seen as an excellent achievement in their eyes, which I understand. When I told my mom what was happening at the printing company, I remember her saying, "I know. It's so awful what they put us through." Bless you, mom. She started working at age nine and was a waitress by the time she was eleven, so she had experienced her share of such things.

Somehow, within the midst of this, I got the idea that I could maybe make a better life for myself. I enrolled in a few classes at the community college. I made it possibly one month that first time before withdrawing. After the printing company, I found myself working in a basement at Sears, which was another awful job, although I did write a lot of poetry during that time, including one of my favorite poems of my life titled "Sears Ladies," which was a tribute to the women I worked with. The Sears job is possibly what pushed me over the edge though. I tried community college again. This time I excelled. Knowing the political context and history of UC Berkeley, it became my dream to transfer there. I worked full-time and attended college full-time with my heart set on Berkeley. In 1991 I transferred there.

My undergraduate years at Berkeley, where I majored in English, were transformative. Although I struggled with the imposter syndrome and was concerned someone would figure out I was not smart enough to be there, I persevered and found ways to successfully navigate the system. I had the wonderful opportunity to often study literature by Black women, including Toni Morrison, Paule Marshall, Maya Angelou, Alice Walker, and Gayle Jones. There are many blessings from this time, including the amazing good fortune I had to be a student of June Jordan's during my senior year.

June, a brilliant poet, activist, essayist, teacher, and so much more, taught a women's studies class that I was able to get a coveted seat in. June demonstrated what I call "life as activism" - how one can be engaged as an activist in daily life. She showed us how living as an activist was important and necessary and something we could all do. I also saw how she aligned herself with the oppressed - whoever was being oppressed regardless of race, ethnicity, religion, gender, or other factors. She also spoke about the importance of truth-telling in one's writing, so

With my *You are Not Alone* collage

truth, imagination, and creativity became forever linked for me, especially within a political context. June introduced us to the activist poet Judy Grahn's *Common Women Poems* that went straight to my heart with their heartfelt and strong portraits of working class women. The political nature of creative expression, which I experienced earlier through the punk rock scene, was magnified as I studied in June's classroom and saw the possibilities for social change through creative work. Through June I would also discover the feminist belief of the personal being political, which I continue to believe.

Another powerful thing is that June believed that everyone can be a poet. Poetry was certainly not something for the elite. She is well-known for a class she taught at Berkeley and in the community titled Poetry for the People. This vision of poetry, being something accessible to everyone, connected with my punk rock DIY belief that everyone can be a musician, artist, writer, and beyond. In June's class I learned so much and she enhanced my understanding of creativity to levels I am still learning about. I believe that all people have creative power and a birthright to express themselves. I also believe everyone has an important story to tell. Thank you for all you gave me and so many others, June! Rest in power.

Berkeley was also my first experience of a solo-home. After living in student cooperative housing for a short period, I got a tiny room above Blondie's Pizza at the intersection of Telegraph and Durant. In my small space with a sink, microwave, and shared bathroom down the hall,

I felt like a millionaire. The room had an old, large window I would push up with my hands to take in the Berkeley streets and the fog rolling over the hills. I sat on the floor of my room making collages and used a metal folding chair and my family's old card table for studying. Late at night I sat with my lamp on in my one-room mansion while reading Morrison, Woolf, Shakespeare, and Chaucer. One of my favorite moments was when my mom visited and we slept on a small mattress on the floor of my little space, sat in cafes together, walked through bookstores, and watched the life of the city from my window. I can easily conjure up memories of how it felt to be in that magical, small room, eating cheap microwavable bean burritos I could purchase in bulk from a market down the street and countless bowls of Top Ramen. I would often walk down College Avenue into the Oakland neighborhood of Rockridge to take in the beautiful houses and gardens and then stop by one of the fabulous bookstores on Telegraph before getting home. In this small, solitary space as a young woman, I cultivated a rich home of learning, creativity, and self-transformation as I dreamed of a future.

In my peaceful home with my *Woman Dreaming of New Poems* collage

My late twenties and early thirties, the years after Berkeley, was another period of self-growth and discovery. I became captivated by the work of Jungian psychoanalyst and writer Clarissa Pinkola Estés who is most famous for writing *Women Who Run with the Wolves: Myths and Stories* of the *Wild Woman Archetype*. This introduced me to new understandings of the imagination, consciousness, and Jungian archetypes. I also read the work of ecofeminists, including Carol J. Adams, Greta Gaard, and Susan Griffin. I fell in love with the large, collaborative art projects of Judy Chicago, specifically *The Dinner Party* and *The Birth Project*, which led to a pilgrimage many years later to view *The Dinner Party* in person once it was permanently installed at the Brooklyn Museum. The work of Frida Kahlo, who I discovered earlier when I was a teenager, was influential and became more prominent for me at this time. Kahlo's art displays a vulnerability and authenticity that has spoken to me throughout my life. Through her self-portraits, I also had my first awareness of how personal expression can take on universal meaning.

This period of my life was also a return to spirituality. I read a good amount of Catholic mysticism and became so enamored by the writings of the late Trappist monk Thomas Merton that I traveled to the Kentucky wilderness near Bardstown for a silent retreat at the monastery where he lived. I also reconnected with the Great Mother and Goddess through the works of Marija Gimbutas and Jungian psychologist Jean Shinoda Bolen. In the midst of these discoveries, I read Thomas Moore's *The Re-enchantment of Everyday Life*, which remains one of my favorite works that led to what I call Everyday Magic, which is the awakening and understanding of daily, "common" activities and rituals as deep and spiritual moments in one's life. During these years of reading and spiritual growth, I had different male partners, but also lived in my second solo-home, an apartment in Fullerton, California. In this apartment, I became captivated by the music of Joni Mitchell. I listened to her *Blue* album countless times. The collages I made at this time of my life were often created using large pieces of discarded cardboard and assorted papers. One I can recall fairly well had a cityscape I drew with thick markers and a woman's figure hovering over the buildings. It was created in the spirit of freedom and independence.

After Berkeley, realizing that it would not be as easy as I thought to make a living as a writer, I worked for many years in counseling jobs, including as a vocational rehabilitation counselor. In the evenings, I would write and make art. I also completed a master's degree in English, but discovered after that it would be difficult for me to find a full-time college-level teaching position without a PhD. I then went back to school to get a second master's degree to become a librarian, a professional career I have now been in for close to twenty years. This gets me up to the period in my life where the title of the book comes from.

One Day I Started a New Life

In my mid thirties, while in the beginning of my career in librarianship, I married for the first time. My husband was a musician. I have good memories of our early times together when I would see him perform at clubs all over Los Angeles. I suppose I longed for a life where I could devote a lot of time to writing and art, so having a partner who did this with music was something I enjoyed. My husband would sometimes have a hot temper that concerned me, but he was working on this with different practices, including yoga. Unfortunately, even though there were stretches of time that gave me hope that things were getting better, I soon found myself in a circular pattern of domestic abuse. I lived as a divided self during this time. To the outside world, I was successful and living a great life as an academic librarian as I worked hard to build up my publication record and other aspects of my professional life to one day secure a tenure-track position. Inside though, I was full of shame and fear. My days were unpredictable. Because of his threats, I also saw no way to escape unless I completely disappeared, gave up my career, and went into hiding. I even hid the abuse for a long time from my mom and brother (my dad passed away before I was married), which was not very hard to do, since they both lived out-of-state and my husband had a lot of charm.

Before this happened to me, I remember thinking that I would never allow a man to abuse me. I imagine I was probably even judgmental of women in such situations, believing I was too strong to ever let that happen to me. I'm embarrassed that I called myself a feminist while having such views that lacked solidarity with other women. I was completely ignorant of the volatility and what happens in domestic abuse situations, including the emotional and psychological toll and the strength it takes to simply survive each day.

One of the painful things that I endured as I tried to figure out an escape, was that some of my beloved possessions would "disappear" when I was at work or out with a friend. I suppose it was a form of punishment. These were not just meaningless possessions. One day it was a set of beautiful dishes my maternal grandmother had given my parents many years ago. Another time it was a pair of vintage blue Lee corduroy overalls, which may seem silly, but they dated back to my undergrad years and I loved them. One day it was many of my beloved books, including ones from Berkeley with my notes in the margins. Within this scary and volatile time, something also happened that made me feel like I was split in two. All of my art I created throughout my twenties and into my thirties was destroyed one day while I was at work. This was almost too much to bear. I do not recall making a conscious decision to no longer make art, but that is what happened for several years. I continued to focus on my writing, teaching, and librarian career – living a divided life and often exhausted with a queasy stomach. It felt like a large pot was boiling on the stove, about to overflow at any minute.

In 2011, I secured the tenure-track position I dreamed of. Within two months, my mom passed away and my situation at home was getting darker and scarier. I'm not sure how I kept moving forward. I had only been in my new position for a few weeks when I experienced a terrifying weekend. Realizing that I may lose my life and that a path to an escape I kept hoping for was not going to miraculously appear, I pulled together all that was left of my inner spirit and I left. I wasn't sure if I would be able to make it to where my car was parked without being discovered and dragged back home, but I made it to my car! I wasn't sure if I would be able to start my car without being detected, but I turned the key in the ignition and began to drive away! Being too afraid of the loud sound I would make closing the car door, I kept the door open, but held onto the handle until I reached the end of the street. I sat in a large parking lot and called my friend. I knew, no matter what happened, even if it meant losing my life, that I wouldn't go back. My husband would be arrested later that day. I entered into a period of police, courts, restraining orders, attorneys, and divorce, but I was free.

For weeks leading up to this moment, I saw an image of myself in my mind. I was sitting alone outside in a nature setting eating an apple in a t-shirt and jeans with tangled, windblown hair. I was peaceful, unafraid, rested, and calm in this image. This image was telling me that losing my career and everything I owned would still be better than staying. I was ready to risk everything for my freedom. On this one day, I started a new life. The following month when I stood in court and testified about what happened to me, my hands and my body shook, but my voice was coming back. I was safe enough to speak my truth. It wouldn't be too long until my art would return.

In my new solo-home, a beautiful one-bedroom loft apartment in Santa Ana, not too far from where I had just started my position at Santa Ana College, I first discovered the wonderful, magnificent ability I now had to sleep whenever I wanted! I wrote a poem titled "In Support of the Violence Against Women Act" where I detail all the places in my apartment and different times I slept. I started going on solo-journeys as a means to rebuild my life. I felt safe during my travels, since I only shared where I was going with my brother and a close friend. I remember thinking that there was no way my ex-husband knew where I was. I also slept so well in those various hotel rooms! During one adventure, I stayed at a wolf sanctuary for two nights and howled with the wolves. I was coming back to myself. And, then, one day, I returned to making art.

I don't recall thinking or saying, "Today I will begin making art again," but that is what happened. What is interesting is that I did not begin small. I went to the art supply store and purchased the largest poster board available. I began to make a mosaic-style collage, a technique I had never done before. This became my *You are Not Alone* collage. When I was at work during this time, I would often see the collage-in-process in my mind. I couldn't wait to get home and stay up late working on it while listening to music and being overcome by the feeling of aliveness. I would go on to make other collages in this style. When I think back on this now, I can clearly see that all of those little pieces of paper I was assembling into one piece was me piecing myself back together. Through the process of creating the collages, I was not only experiencing the rebirth of my art, but my very body and soul. I have never stopped creating art since then. I also returned to making zines, something from my punk rock youth. I have found a great and supportive zine community in the Los Angeles area and beyond.

Once I was on my own, making art, creating zines, and writing in my peaceful, safe space, a dream of buying my first house came over me. I never thought such a thing would be possible in my life, and I was okay with that, since my mom taught me that one can make a beautiful home even in the smallest apartment. With my union position as a community college faculty member, however, the possibility of buying a small home was within reach. I started collecting beautiful books on unique homes, architecture, and interior design. I placed them next to my bed and believed they had a special magic that would lead me to my house. I would go to the Goodwill and different thrift stores and antique shops around where I lived, gathering objects I would place in this future home. This was a wonderful time where I sometimes rode my bike to the shops and brought things home in a basket affixed to the front of my bike or in my backpack. The world felt full of possibilities. Interestingly, many of these objects were round and made of glass. I remember my brother sitting in my apartment and saying, "There are a lot of spheres and orbs in here." This shape has come to symbolize wholeness for me. You will notice circular shapes in much of my art. I also went to used bookstores and found copies of some of the beloved books that were thrown out. They were not my old copies with my notes in the margins, but finding certain editions of these books that I used to own felt like a reclamation and statement of survival. I was gathering beauty and wisdom for my future house.

With my brother David in Sedona, Arizona, around 2013

I received tenure in 2015 at the age of forty-five. The weekend after, I was out looking for my house. After a few failed attempts, I found my two-bedroom home with a large backyard on a purple tree-lined street in Santa Ana. In this home, which has become a place of new growth for my creative life, I tend a wild garden that has been an experiment full of discovery and learning, make art often late into the evening, love and care for rescue dogs who have experienced trauma like me, and continue to always be adding to the overflowing bookshelves and random piles of books. The beautiful objects from the various stores, including the glass orbs, are all here with me.

I remember a powerful moment the first year I was in my house. By this time, I was surprised to find myself in a relationship with a man I deeply loved, although I had not been looking for someone and believed I would remain on my own after all I had been through. We were standing in my new home and he made a gesture toward one of my collages that I had hanging in the hallway. He started, "Now, this…". I remember cutting him off and saying, "No!" since I believed he was going to tell me something negative. He then said, "Wait, let me finish. I don't think this should be hanging in the hallway." I started to feel the old queasiness in my stomach, but then he continued, "This shouldn't be hiding, but be hanging out in the living room, so everyone coming in will see it. This is an artist's house, so her art should be celebrated and displayed prominently."

"An artist's house" ?? "An artist" ??

"Yes," I can now say, "I'm an artist. And this is my peaceful home."

Letting Go of Perfection/Creative Breakthroughs

Over the past decade, since beginning my new life, a wonderful thing happened that allowed me to become more courageous with my art. After returning to collage-making, I decided, rather spontaneously, to take guitar lessons. This led to my ability to let go of perfection more than at any other time before, which I find to be a major creative breakthrough.

On certain nights after work, I sat in a small room in the back of a record shop with Bill Austin, my guitar teacher. Bill was a wonderful mentor. We played guitar together often, but sometimes we would also sit and talk. He gave me advice and shared things about his life. The guitar was very challenging for me. I

At home with Walter and Joni in 2019 (Photo by Steven Soto)

remember first telling Bill that my hands were too small to play and later that my hands were too large. I struggled a lot, but managed to still write some elementary songs with lyrics. I would even sing – not caring how off-key I was. Bill was encouraging. He knew Joni Mitchell was my favorite musician. He believed that I could be playing my basic Joni-inspired tunes in a cafe in a few years if I kept at it.

I enjoyed all I was discovering with the guitar. I would sit on my back porch and sing my tunes with the few basic chords I knew. At a certain point though, I realized that I did not want to put in the time and effort necessary to master the instrument. I was okay with what I learned and not going further. This was new for me. I also discovered that my rudimentary abilities with the guitar were actually enriching my visual art. I started experimenting with different techniques, going to the art supply store often and purchasing new things to try. Being self-taught as an artist was quite liberating, since fumbling around and figuring things out was part of the fun.

Since my revelations with the guitar, I have taken various one-day or short-term classes to just dip in and learn something while being within a creative community. I agree with the idea discussed in David Bayles' and Ted Orland's book *Art & Fear: Observations on the Perils (and Rewards) of Artmaking* (Image Continuum Press) that there are no mistakes when it comes to making art. The process and not the perfection is what I enjoy. I take inspiration from my creative adventures and bring it to my collage paintings and illustrations. I've done short-term explorations with ceramics, loom weaving, improvisational screen printing, basket weaving, intuitive painting, bookmaking, and fabric flower pounding, where you take a hammer and pound flowers into treated fabrics to make gorgeous natural patterns. I have also done something more extensive: I received a sabbatical that allowed me to complete an intense and challenging program to become a certified expressive arts therapist through Expressive Arts Florida Institute. Expressive arts is an intermodal process that involves writing, visual art, dance and movement, drama, sound, and other art forms. There are certified expressive arts therapists, but also others like me who do not have counseling credentials, but practice expressive arts and lead others through the intermodal process for various reasons, including community building and healing.

Living Holistically

After living a divided life for many years, I have worked hard to bring my life together into something more unified. It is my version of living holistically. I don't want to keep my creative life separate from my life as a librarian, because I also don't see my life as a writer and artist as separate from my work at the library. Over the past several years, I've offered artmaking workshops on my campus to student clubs and classes. Most recently, I've been offering expressive arts workshops to faculty and staff. I've also co-coordinated a community poetry reading through the library for many years.

I have been fortunate to receive some recognition for my art over the last decade. I have sold original works. In 2019, at the age of forty-nine, I celebrated my first solo-show. I then had a second solo-show in 2020. My art has been accepted for juried shows and has appeared on book covers. I have authored and illustrated two children's books. I am grateful for all of this.

Building community through art and writing has become one of my greatest passions, including my work with story-gathering projects and encouraging others to tell their stories through art and writing. During my expressive arts training, I was asked to spontaneously sum up my mission and beliefs while completing a class assignment. What came to mind first was, "I believe everyone has an important story to tell." I'll never forget what another student immediately said back to me: "It makes perfect sense that you would say that, because you are a librarian. Libraries are full of stories. When I think of a library, I always think of stories." My heart soared when I heard these words.

Within all this goodness, however, things are not always easy. It is important to share this, because, I believe, in telling our stories, we must be authentic and vulnerable when we feel safe enough to do so. This goes back to the notion of truth-telling I learned from June Jordan. So, here are some of the things I've struggled with. I have been in therapy for years to help me overcome and manage the aftermath of domestic abuse. I was diagnosed with post-traumatic stress disorder. Receiving this diagnosis and understanding what it meant helped immensely in my awareness of what was happening to me and why certain situations filled me with feelings of fear and panic. I can still be triggered and suffer from anxiety, but often I can recognize it and use tools to lessen the suffering. In 2019, I lost my brother to the horrible condition known as ALS or Lou Gehrig's Disease. I now find myself in the world without my family of origin or children of my own. I will glide through long stretches of joy and then encounter a patch of dark thoughts and horrible loneliness. Yet, even in the midst of this, I carry on.

At home with Jack and Lily in 2023 (Photo by Mario Arreola)

Art is at the center of my ability to be resilient. In this book, I offer my creative journey through images, but it is much more than that. The images found here are about my survival and transformation. I tell stories through my art, including my own story. I hope you will find something that also resonates with your life and any struggles you have endured. I also hope something will connect with the joy, adventure, wonder, love, and happiness you have experienced. Everything included in this book came to be because one day I found the courage to start a new life.

COLLAGE AND MIXED MEDIA

Works selected for this section begin with the first collage I made in 2013 (*You Are Not Alone*) when I returned to making visual art and continue through 2023. My collage-making in 2013 began with mosaic-style creations that were created solely with glue and recycled magazine and book paper on cardboard or poster board. Over the years, I began to use different materials, including acrylic paint, watercolor paint, watercolor pencils, and pen. I have also experimented with wood, canvas, lokta paper, art boards, and various other papers. One of the elements of collage and mixed media work that I love is the physical experience of working with my hands and feeling the different textures beneath my fingers as the art is created. I believe this also contributes to the healing and therapeutic nature of artmaking because it is an embodied and handmade practice. I create almost all of my art standing at the kitchen counter, which feels like the heart of my home.

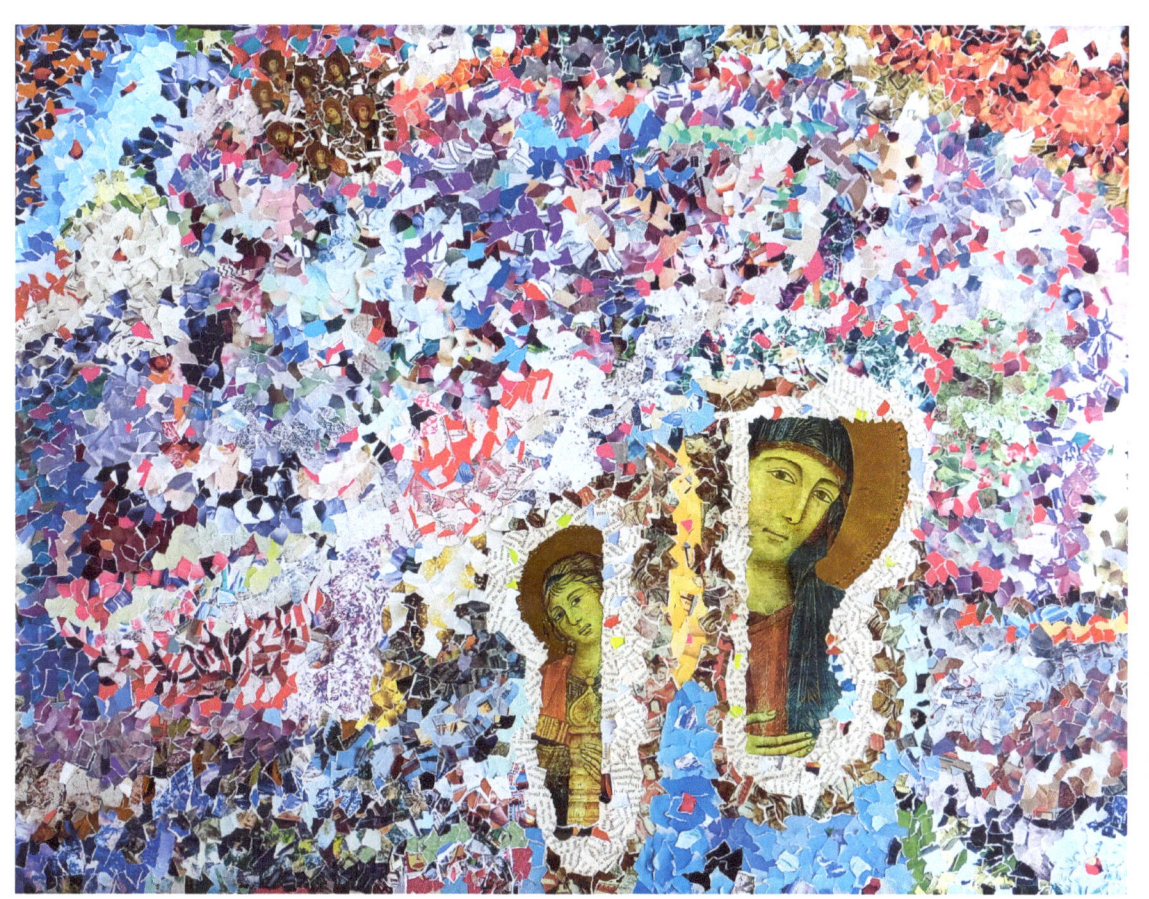

STACY RUSSO

You Are Not Alone, 30 x 40, magazine paper and discarded book paper on cardboard, 2013

above:
Double Goddess, 24 x 36, magazine paper and discarded book paper on cardboard, 2013

Opposite:
Daydreaming at Home in My Chair, 18.5 x 15, magazine paper on cardboard, 2015
Daydreaming at Home in My Chair 2, 18.5 x 15, magazine paper on cardboard, 2015

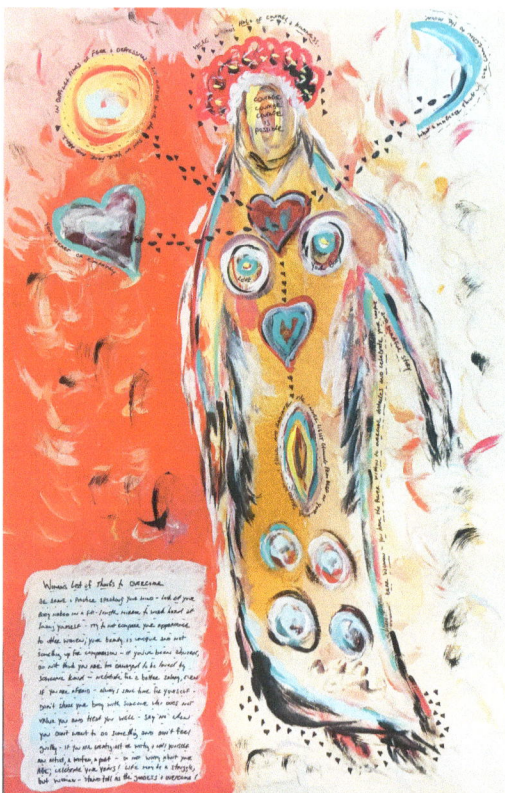

Woman's List of Things to Overcome, 30 x 20, acrylic paint and marker on cold press illustration board, 2015

Woman's List of Things to Overcome

Be brave & practice speaking your mind - Look at your body naked in a full-length mirror to work hard at loving yourself - Try to not compare your appearance to other women; your beauty is unique and not something up for comparison - If you've been abused, do not think you are too damaged to be loved by someone kind - Negotiate for a better salary, even if you are afraid - Always save time for yourself - Don't share your body with someone who does not value you and treat you well - Say "no" when you don't want to do something and don't feel guilty - If you are creating art or writing, call yourself an artist, a writer, a poet - Do not worry about your age; celebrate your years! - Life may be a struggle, but woman - stand tall as the Goddess & overcome!

Woman's List of Beautiful Food, 30 x 20, acrylic paint and marker on cold press illustration board, 2015

Woman's List of Beautiful Food

Cherries - Blueberries - Strawberries - Onions - Pears - Water - Wine - Dark Chocolate - Brown Rice - Almonds - Avocados - Apples - Blueberries - Peanut Butter - Peas - Pineapple - Mangoes - The Sun - Wind - Moon - Tomatoes - Garlic - Rosemary - Oregano - Lavender - Bell Peppers - Coffee (Yes! Yes!) - Kale - Squash - Potatoes - Olive Oil - Cinnamon - Ginger - Basil - Oatmeal - Vanilla - Apples - Oranges - Lemon - Limes - Grapes - Grapefruit - Pecans - Walnuts - All Things Organic & Fair Trade - Pinto Beans - Black Beans - Plums - Peaches - Nectarines - Watermelon - Pasta - Coconuts - Bananas - Music - Poetry - Your Lover's Body - Olives - Pistachios - Jalapenos - Eggplant - Corn - Breads - Apricots - Pumpkins - Pomegranates - Carrots - May All Beings Know Peace

Woman's List of Heroines, 30 x 20, acrylic paint and marker on cold press illustration board, 2015

Woman's List of Heroines

Frida Kahlo - bell hooks - June Jordan - Judy Chicago - Patti Smith - Joni Mitchell - Clarissa Pinkola Estés - Virginia Woolf - Peace Pilgrim - Faith Wilding - Sandra Cisneros - Alice Walker - Judy Grahn - Dorothy Day - Jane Goddall - Carol J. Adams - Carolyn Helibrun - Alice Koller - Maxine Hong Kingston - Zora Neale Hurston - Natalie Goldberg - Annie Knight - Theresa Paulsrud - Amber Garza - Amy Keller - Deanna Van Ligten - Marion Woodman - Jean Shinoda Bolen - May Sarton - Wanda Coleman - Anne Sexton - Audre Lorde - Gerda Lerner - Carolyn Merchant - Anais Nin - Tillie Olsen - Adrienne Rich - Isabel Allende - Susan Griffin - Elaine Showalter - Starhawk - Gloria Anzaldúa - Joan Mitchell - Marina Abramović - Alice Neel - Betye Saar - Fiona Apple - Phoebe Snow - Joan Armatrading - Hildegard of Bingen - Sappho

Woman's List of Love Activism, 30 x 20, acrylic paint and marker on cold press illustration board, 2015

Woman's List of Love Activism

For You - Community - All Living Beings - Earth

Listen mindfully - Create art & music - Support others' creativity - Be minimalistic & reject careless consumerism - Rest when you are tired - Read books/support libraries - Garden - Slow down - Take walks - Ride a bike - Start a community reading group - Take warm baths - Reject violence - Capture & release insects - Buy vegan & cruelty free cleaning supplies & cosmetics - Laugh, sing, and dance - Smile at strangers - Buy fair trade coffee & chocolate - Support local businesses - Bring food to the poor - Reject what does not nourish your soul - Write poetry - Visit the ill - Reject racist & sexist jokes - Be a vegan feminist - Visit museums - Meditate - Repair something instead of throwing it away - See others with the eye of your heart

Woman's List for Troubled Times, 30 x 20, acrylic paint and marker on cold press illustration board, 2015

Woman's List for Troubled Times

Be thankful for blueberries - Plant a grapefruit tree - Ride your bike to the ocean (Fuck, yeah!) - Eat an avocado at the ocean while wrapped in a blanket - Sit outside with the sun on your face - Take a warm salt bath with your hands resting on your belly - Collage - Paint - Allow yourself to go to bed and cry, cry, cry - Chocolate in bed - Chocolate at 1 a.m. - Chocolate for breakfast - Dream of where you will travel next - Eat something that makes your belly feel warm - Walk barefoot in the grass - Tell someone you trust that you are sad - Be thankful for all the times you were loved and when your love was received and cherished - Place the palm of your hand on your heart and whisper hope, hope, hope - Only drink from beautiful ceramic and glass cups - Repair something - Believe in tomorrow

STACY RUSSO

Clockwise from top left: *Women Gathering to Create Beauty*, 10 x 8, acrylic paint and magazine paper on art board, 2018. *Women Gathering to Create Beauty* is the cover art for the poetry collection *What Happened Was:* by Anna Leahy (Small Harbor Publishing, 2021); *Storytellers (Women's Wisdom Gathering)*, 10 x 8, acrylic paint and magazine paper on art board, 2018. *Storytellers (Women's Wisdom Gathering)* is the cover art for my book *A Better World Starts Here: Activists and Their Work* (Sanctuary Publishers, 2019); *Women on a Pilgrimage (Women Traveling)*, 10 x 8, acrylic paint and magazine paper on art board, 2018; *Women Celebrating Their Survival and Remembering Those Who Didn't Survive*, 10 x 8, acrylic paint and magazine paper on art board, 2018

ONE DAY I STARTED A NEW LIFE

Visiting with My Brother, Orlando, Florida, October 2018, 30 x 20, acrylic paint and magazine paper on lokta paper, 2018

My brother was diagnosed with the terrible condition known as ALS or Lou Gehrig's Disease around 2016. While visiting him in late 2018 when he was receiving hospice care at home, I sat next to his bed and cut out various images from magazines. At this time, he was unable to speak or use any part of his body except for some movement in his toes and a few fingers, but he no longer had enough strength or control to type or make gestures. We communicated through other means such as presence. When I returned home to California after that visit, I assembled this collage from the images I cut out and gathered by his bedside. My brother passed away in January 2019 at the age of 57. He was an amazing person who was loved by many. For me, he represented unconditional love and he was a great support for my writing and art. After his passing, I entered a difficult time since he was the last member of my immediate family here on Earth. Art has been one of the healing forces for me to navigate this new terrain where I did not imagine I would find myself. Images I have created that represent my Spirit Family, some of which are included in this section, have been one important and helpful form of therapy.

Above:
I Walked Away and Started a New Life, 22 x 17, watercolor paint and magazine paper on paper, 2019

I Walked Away and Started a New Life is the cover art for the short fiction collection *A Brief Natural History of Women* by Sarah Freligh (Small Harbor Publishing, 2023).

Following page spread:
Flying Home to California, My View from the Plane, 30 x 20, acrylic paint and magazine paper, map paper, and discarded book paper on lokta paper, 2019

ONE DAY I STARTED A NEW LIFE

Left to right:
Imaginary Garden Library, 12 x 9, watercolor paint, acrylic paint, pen, magazine paper, newspaper, and old dictionary paper on mixed media paper, 2019

Imaginary Goddess Library, 12 x 9, watercolor paint, acrylic paint, pen, magazine paper, and newspaper on mixed media paper, 2019

Imaginary Map Library, 12 x 9, watercolor paint, acrylic paint, watercolor pencils, magazine paper, newspaper, and map paper on mixed media paper, 2019

Librarian at Work, 12 x 9, acrylic paint, magazine paper, newspaper, and pen on mixed media paper, 2019

STACY RUSSO

ONE DAY I STARTED A NEW LIFE

Above:
Gathering Beauty in the Storm, 17 x 22, watercolor paint, magazine paper, and old dictionary paper on art paper, 2019

Opposite:
Answering the Call, 12 x 9, watercolor paint, watercolor pencils, magazine paper, and pen on mixed media paper, 2019

ONE DAY I STARTED A NEW LIFE

Above:
The Revolution Will Be Colorful, 22 x 17, watercolor paint, magazine paper, and pen on art paper, 2019

Opposite:
Follow Your Bliss, 22 x 17, watercolor paint, magazine paper, and pen on art paper, 2019

Grow Your Garden (Urban Garden), 22 x 17, watercolor paint and assorted recycled paper on art paper, 2019

ONE DAY I STARTED A NEW LIFE

Above:
She Returned to Her True Self, 14.5 x 11, watercolor paint, watercolor pencils, plain paper, pen, and magazine paper on old book paper, 2019

Opposite:
This is My Life Happening Right Now, 14.5 x 11, watercolor paint, watercolor pencils, plain paper, pen, and magazine paper on old book paper, 2019

Sometimes you need to remind yourself, "This is my life happening right now," get dressed up like a beautiful flower, and raise your arms toward the sun.

ONE DAY I STARTED A NEW LIFE

Everyday Saints, 14.5 x 11, watercolor paint, watercolor pencils, plain paper, pen, and magazine paper on old book paper, 2019

The Years Fly By, 12 x 9, watercolor paint, watercolor pencils, pen, and magazine paper on mixed media paper, 2019

My Brother Loved to Fly, Now He Flies in Heaven, 24 x 18, watercolor paint, acrylic paint, aeronautical chart, old geometry textbook paper, magazine paper, and pen on mixed media paper, 2020

Full Moon Sky, 24 x 18, watercolor pencils, colored pencils, and magazine paper on mixed media paper, 2020

ONE DAY I STARTED A NEW LIFE

Woman Dreaming of New Poems, 24 x 18, acrylic paint, watercolor pencils, and magazine paper on mixed media paper, 2020

Earth & Sky, 24 x 18, watercolor paint, watercolor pencils, pen, and magazine paper on mixed media paper, 2020

ONE DAY I STARTED A NEW LIFE

Above:
How Freedom Feels, 10 x 8, watercolor paint, pen, and magazine paper on art board, 2019

How Freedom Feels is the cover art for a collection of essays I edited titled *Feminist Pilgrimage: Journeys of Discovery* (Litwin Books, 2020).

Opposite:
Women's Secret Tent, 17 x 22, watercolor paint, pen, and recycled paper on art paper, 2019

When You Think of Me, Think of Me Wild and Free, 22 x 17, watercolor paint, pen, lokta and assorted paper, and magazine paper on art paper, 2019

You Can Find Me at Home Reading, 24 x 18, watercolor paint and magazine paper on mixed media paper, 2021

Nina's Book, 10 x 8, watercolor paint, pen, and magazine paper on art board, 2020

Nina's Book is the cover art for the poetry collection *Our Mother of Sorrows* by Nina Clements (Urban Farmhouse Press, 2020).

The People of Los Angeles Wake to Find the Freeways Covered in Beautiful Flowers, 22 x 17, watercolor paint, pen, and magazine paper on art paper, 2020

Garden from Above, 22 x 18, watercolor paint, pen, hemp yarn, and assorted paper on mixed media paper, 2020

Garden in Bloom, 12 x 17, acrylic paint, yarn, and magazine paper on grocery bag, 2021

Hermitage, 9 x 12, watercolor paint, watercolor pencils, pen and magazine paper on mixed media paper, 2020

What a Life is For, 17 x 22, watercolor paint, watercolor pencils, pen, magazine paper, old dictionary paper, and lokta paper on art paper, 2021

My Favorite Bookstores, 8 x 10, watercolor paint, watercolor pencils, pen, and magazine paper on art board, 2020

Moving to California in 1981, 14 x 11, watercolor paint, watercolor pencils, magazine paper, pen, map paper on mixed media paper, 2021

ONE DAY I STARTED A NEW LIFE

Henry Miller Library, Big Sur, From Memory, 8 x 10, watercolor paint, watercolor pencils, pen, and magazine paper on art board, 2020

My Berkeley Studio, 1993, Age 23, 11 x 14, watercolor paint, watercolor pencils, pen, and magazine paper on mixed media paper, 2020

Poetry Reading, 10 x 10, watercolor paint, watercolor pencils, pen, and magazine paper on mixed media paper, 2020

The Goddess Spaceship Comes to Earth, 18 x 24, watercolor paint, pen, and magazine paper on mixed media paper, 2020

Growing Up in Southern California in the 1980s, 10 x 10, watercolor paint, pen, and magazine paper on mixed media paper, 2020

Fender's Ballroom, Long Beach, California, in the 1980s, 11 x 14, watercolor paint, pen, and magazine paper on mixed media paper, 2020

Above:
Punks for Peace, 11 x 14, watercolor paint, acrylic paint, watercolor pencils, pen, and magazine paper on mixed media paper, 2021

Opposite:
Plant Sale, 18 x 24, watercolor paint, pen, and magazine paper on mixed media paper, 2020

The Small House with the Wild Garden, 20 x 30, watercolor paint, watercolor pencils, acrylic paint, lokta paper, magazine paper, and pen on poster board, 2022

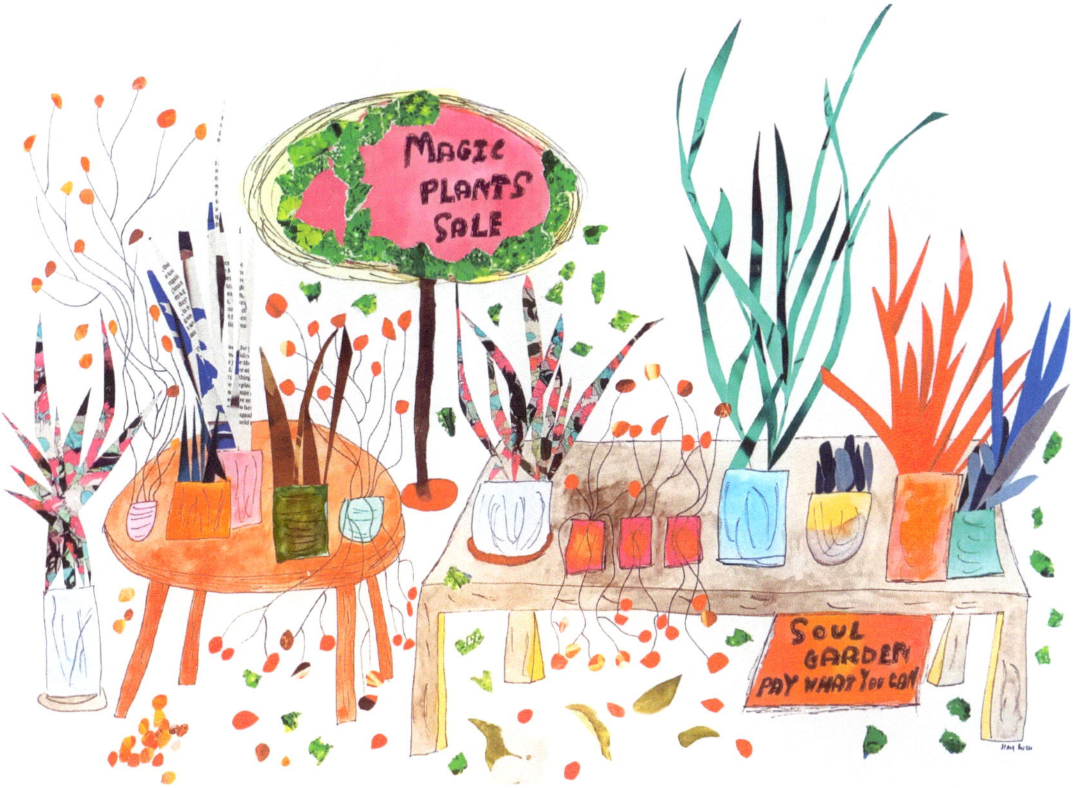
MAGIC PLANTS SALE
SOUL GARDEN PAY WHAT YOU CAN

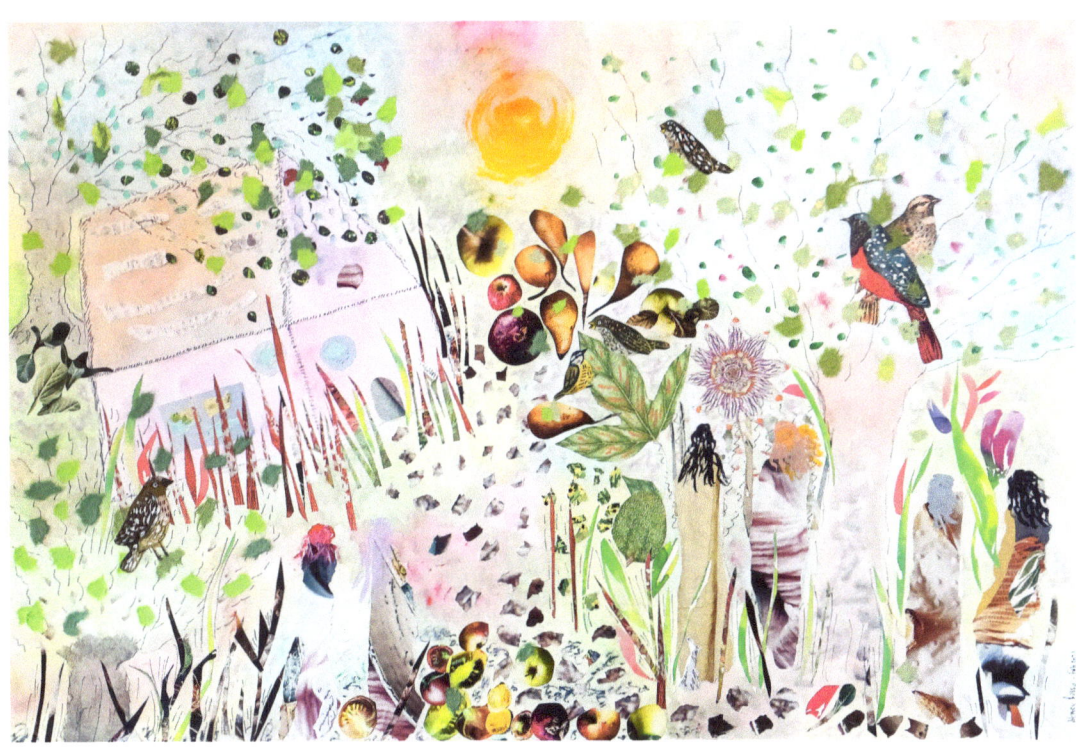

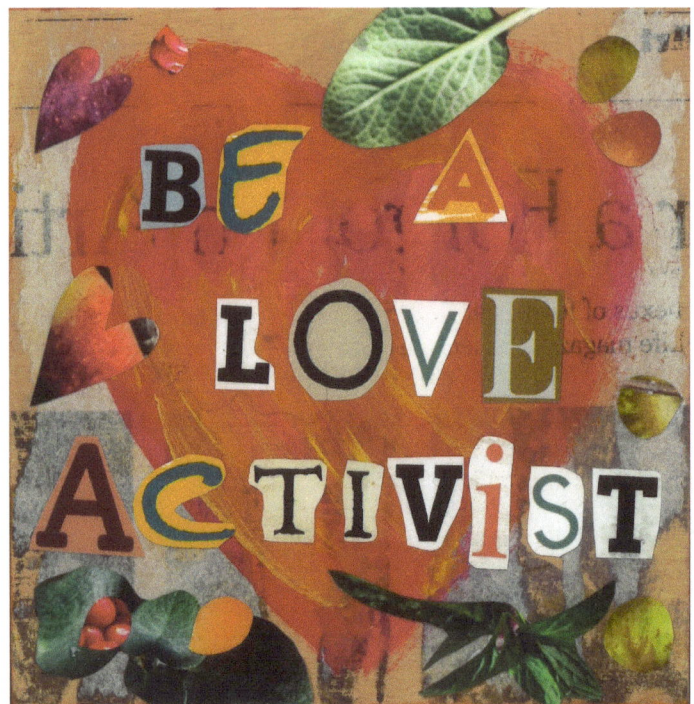

Be a Love Activist, 4 x 4, acrylic paint, newspaper, and magazine paper on wood, 2021
Be Brave Love Powerfully, 4 x 4, acrylic paint, newspaper, and magazine paper on wood, 2021

Around 2014 I started to think deeply about the relationship between love and activism that resulted in a form of daily activism I call "Love Activism." I made some art around this idea, a pamphlet, and later a book (*Love Activism*, Litwin Books). The Love Activism art I have created since this time has mostly been mixed media on wood with different sayings, such as "Be a Love Activist," "Be Brave Love Powerfully," "Celebrate Your Unique Beauty," and "Forever Feminist." To get the textured background, I press the wood blocks into newspaper when the paint is still wet. I let it sit for just a few minutes and pull the wood off, which results in varied patterns and sometimes words and images from the paper. I then create layers of art against this background. In the past I have sold the small Love Activism wood pieces at art and zine festivals and in different stories in Southern California and Taos, New Mexico.

Walking Meditation, 20 x 30, watercolor paint, acrylic paint, pen, lokta paper, and magazine paper on poster board, 2022

ONE DAY I STARTED A NEW LIFE

Above:
Desert Walk, 11 x 14, watercolor paint, watercolor pencils, pen, and magazine paper on mixed media paper, 2022

Opposite:
Ocean Walk, 11.5 x 17, acrylic paint, pen, watercolor pencils, plain paper, magazine paper, and newspaper on grocery bag, 2022

Stitching, Mending, 14.5 x 12, acrylic paint, pen, yarn, newspaper, and magazine paper on grocery bag, 2022

ONE DAY I STARTED A NEW LIFE

Above:
Barefoot Librarian, 8,5 x 5.5, watercolor paint, watercolor pencils, lokta paper, pen, and magazine paper on mixed media paper, 2021

Opposite:
What I Found There, 19.5 x 10.5, acrylic paint, old dictionary paper, and magazine paper on reclaimed wood, 2022

ONE DAY I STARTED A NEW LIFE

Above:
Musicians & Artists, 22 x 17, watercolor paint, pen, and magazine paper on art paper, 2020

Opposite:
When You Come By, I'll Be Out in the Garden, 11 x 14, watercolor paint, watercolor pencils, pen, and magazine paper on mixed media paper, 2022

Above:
Rena's World, 24 x 18, watercolor paint, acrylic paint, colored pencils, and magazine paper on mixed media paper, 2020

Dancer, 14 x 11, watercolor pencils, magazine paper, alcohol ink, and pen on mixed media paper, 2021

Opposite:
Darling, Hold My Calls, 19 x 12.5, watercolor paint, acrylic paint, pen, lokta paper, and magazine paper on art paper, 2023

You Give Me My Daily Poetry, 19 x 12.5, watercolor paint, pen, and magazine paper on art paper, 2022

Do You Ever Think of Me Like I Think of You?, 19 x 12.5, watercolor paint, acrylic paint, pen, and magazine paper on art paper, 2022

Finding My Way, 12.5 x 19, watercolor paint, pen, plain paper, bookstore receipts, and magazine paper on art paper, 2022

The Lovers, 19 x 12.5, watercolor paint and magazine paper on art paper, 2023

Nina and Stacy, 19 x 12.5, watercolor paint, pen, and magazine paper on art paper, 2023

ONE DAY I STARTED A NEW LIFE

Above:
Sunday Morning, 12.5 x 19, watercolor paint, pen, and magazine paper on art paper, 2022

Opposite:
Possibilities, 19 x 12.5, watercolor paint, pen, acrylic paint, and magazine paper on art paper, 2022

Above and right:
Everyone I've Lost is Still with Me, 17 x 19.5, watercolor paint, pen, and magazine paper on mixed media paper, 2023

Hello, Spirit Family, 19 x 12.5, watercolor paint, acrylic paint, pen, and magazine paper on art paper, 2022

Opposite:
Taking Off in My Flying Suit, 19 x 12.5, acrylic paint, plain paper, watercolor paint, watercolor pencils, pen, and magazine paper on art paper, 2023

ONE DAY I STARTED A NEW LIFE

Above:
With My Spirit Family, 24 x 18, acrylic paint and magazine paper on mixed media paper, 2023

Wearing My Magical, Healing Coat, 24 x 18, acrylic paint, watercolor pencils, pen, and magazine paper on mixed media paper, 2023

Opposite:
In My Dad's Magical Garden, 18 x 24, acrylic paint, watercolor paint, watercolor pencils, pen, and magazine paper on mixed media paper, 2023

Above:
Book Women, 11 x 11, acrylic paint, watercolor paint, pen, magazine paper, on art paper, 2023

Opposite:
Peace Walk by the Ocean, 32 x 46, acrylic paint, magazine paper, and dictionary paper on canvas, 2023
Walking with Wolves, 24 x 36, acrylic paint and magazine paper on canvas, 2023

STACY RUSSO

MIXED MEDIA MEMOIR

A few years after returning to artmaking I began to combine autobiography and visual art in a more deliberate way by creating an image tied directly to a single memory or longer experience and then writing words on the artwork. In this section of mixed media memoir my life as a writer and artist are combined in perhaps the most evident way. Visual storytelling like this is many things, including tributes and celebrations. It is possibly the most vulnerable form of visual art I create, since I am sharing parts of my life story in a direct manner.

Places from Memory, 14 x 11, watercolor paint, watercolor pencils, and magazine paper on mixed media paper, 2020

Top: Driving to Mendocino, California, 2006; My Grandma's Magical Apartment, Harrisburg, PA, 1979 - Middle: Sedona, Arizona, 2014; Sacred Mountain, Taos, New Mexico, 2012 - Bottom: My Berkeley, California, Studio, 1992; Oregon Coast, 2013

Above:
My Grandma's Magical Apartment, 11 x 14, watercolor paint, watercolor pencils, and magazine paper on mixed media paper, 2020

1. My grandma's apartment was on Market Street in the heart of Harrisburg, PA. You had to walk up several steep flights of stairs to reach her apt on the top floor. When you got close, you could smell her burning rose incense. 2. Her apartment had amazing furniture and two windows that looked out to the city and the sidewalk below. My brother and I loved to hang out with her. 3. She had a tiny kitchen and she ate simple meals like toast and black coffee. 4. She kept strange scrapbooks full of bizarre news clippings and she liked to watch boxing on her small TV.

Opposite:
My Dad's Magical Garden, 12.5 x 9.75, watercolor pencils, magazine paper, and pen on old book paper, 2020

In the 1970s my family lived in a small house with a magnificent garden in Mechanicsburg, Pennsylvania. Although my dad had little formal education beyond grade school, he was a master with deep knowledge of the earth, seeds, planting, & harvesting. This is an intuitive & patient wisdom that comes through the heart & soul and moves within one's hands in the soil.

David Shotsberger's Magical Garden

99 ...

100 *North-American Indian clay figure, Missouri, U.S.A.*

101 *Tattooed ... from the Kasai r... ...ica*

102 *Wooden Bambara idol, Africa*

103 *Fetishes of the Wakwere, Africa*

104 *Bambara goddess of fertility, Africa*

105 *Fetish of the Fang Tribes, Africa*

106 *Terra-cotta figures in the Jalisco style of Mexico*

107 *Clay figures of the Huaxtecs, Mexico*

108 *Bronze Age idols, Sweden*

... *Ashanti goddesses of fertility, Africa*

... *...inted figures from the Caraja Indians, Brazil*

My Dad's Magical Garden

In the 1970s my family lived in a small house with a magnificent garden in Mechanicsburg, Pennsylvania. Although my dad had little formal education beyond grade school, he was a master with deep knowledge of the earth, seeds, planting + harvesting. This is an intuitive + patient wisdom that comes through the heart + soul and moves within one's hands in the soil.

With My Mom at Work, 11 x 14, watercolor paint, watercolor pencils, pen, and magazine paper on mixed media paper, 2020

When I was a little girl, my mom worked as a janitor, cleaning the public school district building. Sometimes she took me with her. She would put me in the chairs of the big administrators and spin me around. No one was there except us two and it felt magical. My mom set me up at a desk with rocks from around the building & paint & I would sit there & decorate them.

Playing Cards with My Dad, 11 x 14, watercolor paint, watercolor pencils, pen, and magazine paper on mixed media paper, 2020

When I was in elementary school in the 1970s and I got old enough to count & bluff, my dad taught me to play poker and blackjack. On the weekends or after work if he wasn't too tired, we would sit at the kitchen table and play cards. I used pennies for betting that I kept in an old Folger's coffee jar.

ONE DAY I STARTED A NEW LIFE

Growing Up Punk Rock, 14.5 x 11.1, watercolor paint, watercolor pencils, plain paper, magazine paper, and pen on old book paper, 2020

In the 1980s I was a Southern California punk rock girl. I got in a lot of trouble and had a blast! I'm thankful for my wild punk rock youth.

Circus Protest, 11.1 x 14.5, watercolor paint, watercolor pencils, plain paper, magazine paper, and pen on old book paper, 2020

I became politically active as a teenager. This included animal rights. Once I joined a protest against the circus with my friends. We got around to the back of the property where some of the animals were kept. There were several elephants under an outdoor makeshift structure. They had chains around their ankles and could not move much. They were so far from home. A man holding a metal pipe & smoking a cigarette was watching them. He looked tattered, weathered, and had missing teeth. We tried to talk to him. At the time, I think I felt mostly anger & disgust toward the man, but now, many years later, I can feel those emotions mixed with empathy for him. He looked like someone the world had given up on, being possibly caught up in the violent cycle of economic survival & cruelty. The circus show went on for several days. Some of us witnessed the horrors behind the curtain.

ONE DAY I STARTED A NEW LIFE

Encountering the Goddess, 11.1 x 14.5, watercolor paint, watercolor pencils, plain paper, magazine paper, and pen on old book paper, 2020

When I was a young woman around age 21, I went to the Los Angeles County Museum of Art (LACMA). In one area that felt underground I discovered ancient Goddess figurines. I was captivated and felt good all over. Some of the Goddesses were thin and others were round with large hips and breasts. I was overwhelmed seeing women's bodies venerated. It was affirming and life-changing. After this experience, I returned often to the museum. I enjoyed sitting at the cafe drinking coffee close to the Goddesses.

Above:
Professor VèVè Clark's Magical Classroom for "Caribbean Literature by Women," Wheeler Hall, UC Berkeley, 1992, 11 x 14, watercolor paint, watercolor pencils, magazine paper, and pen on mixed media paper, 2021

Following spread:
Going to Berkeley, 1991, 9.5 x 12, watercolor paint, watercolor pencils, plain paper, magazine paper, and pen on old book paper, 2020

Studying English at UC Berkeley was a life-changing and beautiful experience. The community surrounding the campus with its cafes, art, music, and bookstores was heavenly. I love to daydream & reminisce. Still, my story would not be complete or honest if I didn't share that I also struggled profoundly with what I now know is the "Imposter Phenomenon." I arrived at Berkeley from the community college where I attended full-time while working full-time in various hell jobs. My parents didn't go to college, so I didn't really know how to navigate things. I felt scrappy & different from many of my classmates. I read every page assigned & more, since I was afraid of being "found out" that I wasn't smart enough to be there. I believed my grammar or speaking style would reveal something, so I often remained silent. These fears followed me through my first master's degree even though I was top of my class. All of this somehow doesn't cast a shadow for me. I made it. Berkeley is magnificent and mine.

ONE DAY I STARTED A NEW LIFE

Going to Berkeley, 1991

Studying English at UC Berkeley was a life-changing & beautiful experience. The community surrounding the campus with its cafes, art, music, & bookstores was heavenly. I love to daydream & reminisce. Still, my story would not be complete or honest if I didn't share that I also struggled profoundly with what I now know is the "Imposter Phenomenon." I arrived at Berkeley from the community college where I attended full-time while working full-time in various hell jobs. My parents didn't go to college, so I didn't really know how to navigate things. I felt scrappy & different from many of my classmates. I read every page assigned & more, since I was afraid of being "found out" that I wasn't smart enough to be there. I believed my grammar or speaking style would reveal something, so I often remained silent. These fears followed me through my first master's degree even though I was top of my class. All of this somehow doesn't cast a shadow for me. I made it. Berkeley is magnificent & mine.

Becoming a Librarian, 12.5 x 9.7, watercolor paint, watercolor pencils, plain paper, magazine paper, recycled library catalog cards, and pen on old book paper, 2020

When I was 32, I went back to school to get a second master's degree to become a librarian. I love research, books, periodicals, & writing, and I wanted to make a living serving and helping people. I also longed for an academic life working on a college campus around students all day and colleagues who are passionate about teaching, writing, and the arts. I've been an academic librarian now for 15 years. P.S. Librarians don't just read all day.

Woman Who Runs with the Wolves, 14.5 x 11, watercolor paint, watercolor pencils, plain paper, magazine paper, and pen on old book paper, 2020

I've always loved wolves. So did my brother. Maybe we were influenced by my mom. She loved them too and would even play a recording of soft jazz with wolves howling. I think it was called "Jazz Wolf." In my early 40s I traveled to Montana to visit a wolf sanctuary. I stayed for 2 nights and on the morning I was leaving a dream came true! I howled with a wolf pack!

ONE DAY I STARTED A NEW LIFE

Solo Monastery Journey, 9.7 x 12.5, watercolor paint, watercolor pencils, plain paper, magazine paper, and pen on old book paper, 2020

Around age 32, I traveled to Kentucky to stay at the Abbey of Gethsemani, the monastery where the famous monk Thomas Merton lived. I flew into Louisville, rented a pick-up truck, and drove into the Kentucky wilderness to the monastery near Bardstown. I stayed for 5 nights & spent most of my time walking around the grounds, but one day the silence got to me & I drove the truck to Cincinnati & back, playing loud music & drinking a vanilla latte from a city cafe.

Around age 32, I traveled to Kentucky to stay at the Abbey of Gethsemani, the monastery where the famous monk Thomas Merton had lived. I flew into Louisville, rented a pick-up truck, and drove out into the Kentucky wilderness to the monastery near Bardstown. I stayed for 5 nights & spent most of my time walking around the grounds, but one day the silence got to me & I drove the truck to Cincinnati + back, playing loud music + drinking a vanilla latte from a city cafe.

JOURNEY

Rebirth, 14.5 x 11, watercolor paint, watercolor pencils, acrylic paint, plain paper, magazine paper, and pen on old book paper, 2020

Around age 34, someone who I believed loved me destroyed all of the art I made throughout my life, including beloved ones. When I discovered what happened, I felt ill & split in 2. I entered into several dark years with more cruelty & sadness. I continued with my writing & professional career & was often complimented on my success, but fear & shame were my secret companions. I no longer made collages. I was half-alive. At age 41, I moved alone into a beautiful loft apartment in Santa Ana, California. One day I started making a large collage on a piece of cardboard. I worked on the collage after work for several weeks and felt full of joy using my hands to tear, cut, & assemble hundreds of small pieces of paper. Since then, I have never stopped. At age 48, I celebrated my 2 first solo shows. In the darkest nights, we can't see a path or way to escape, but at some moment an opportunity may appear to be re-born. When that moment comes, we must be ready to say "Yes!"

Freedom, 14.5 x 11, watercolor paint, watercolor pencils, plain paper, magazine paper, and pen on old book paper, 2020

I love New Mexico. Not too long after my divorce, I travelled to Taos & stayed at the magical Mabel Dodge Luhan House. One day I was looking at a map & discovered Colorado was not too far away, so I drove there. I reached Colorado on a 2-lane road with nothing around except mountains & a big blue sky. I pulled the car over, got out, and put my arms up in the air & let out a loud & amazing yell. I heard my voice echo against the mountains. I laughed & put my arms up again and yelled as loud as I could several times. Freedom.

Above:
Wild Librarian Bakery, 14.5 x 11, watercolor paint, watercolor pencils, plain paper, magazine paper, and pen on old book paper, 2020

For a few years I had a permit through the County for a home bakery called the Wild Librarian Bakery! I created treats like the Pablo Neruda Coconut Love Cupcake, named after my favorite poet, and the On the Road chocolate cupcake inspired by Kerouac. I sold the baked goods along with my poems & artwork at festivals and I even baked for a vegan/vegetarian restaurant! This started a dream of opening a real place called the Wild Library Bakery! I imagined it as a bakery with a bookstore. There would be poetry readings, book clubs, & art workshops!

Opposite:
My Ritual Walk, 14.5 x 11, watercolor paint, watercolor pencils, plain paper, magazine paper, and pen on old book paper, 2020

1. One of my joys of my life is that I have a ritual walk. It's a walk I've taken almost annually for nearly 30 years as a pilgrimage. The walk starts on College Avenue near the UC Berkeley campus and travels through Berkeley to the wondrous neighborhood of Rockridge in Oakland. 2. When I do this walk, I feel it is one with my body & soul. Some things have come and gone over the years, but others have remained the same. It all carries on. Just like life. I can daydream whenever I desire and imagine myself there on that magical path.

My Ritual Walk

① One of the joys of my life is that I have a ritual walk. It's a walk I've taken almost annually for nearly 30 years as a pilgrimage. The walk starts on College Avenue near the UC Berkeley campus and travels through Berkeley to the wondrous neighborhood of Rockridge in Oakland.

② When I do this walk, I feel it is one with my body & soul. Some things have come and gone over the years, but others have remained the same. It all carries on, just like life. I can daydream whenever I desire and imagine myself there on that magical path.

Women's Retreat, 12.5 x 9.7, watercolor paint, watercolor pencils, plain paper, and pen on old book paper, 2020

Around age 42 I went to a women's retreat in Sedona, Arizona. We wrote together, meditated, and walked. One night we shared a silent meal. It was a transformative experience that gave me courage with my art & writing.

Pilgrimage to The Dinner Party, 12.5 x 9.7, watercolor paint, watercolor pencils, plain paper, magazine paper, and pen on old book paper, 2020

Several years ago I traveled to the Brooklyn Art Museum to see Judy Chicago's legendary feminist art creation: The Dinner Party. I stayed in a beautiful artist's studio not far from the museum. While in NY, I also visited the Museum of Modern Art, Poets House Library (wow!), Bluestockings Bookstore (hell, yeah!) and other amazing bookstores, and ate a lot of great vegan food. I also got to spend a whole day with a wonderful friend & photographer. Thank you, New York!

Poets House, 12.5 x 9.7, watercolor paint, watercolor pencils, plain paper, and pen on old book paper, 2020

During my trip to NYC, I visited Poets House along the Hudson River. It is home to an amazing poetry library with over 70,000 books & other items. It was a dream to visit this magical place as a poet librarian! Heart soar feeling!

Guitar Lessons, 12 x 8.5, watercolor paint, watercolor pencils, acrylic paint, magazine paper, plain paper, and pen on musical score, 2020

Around age 42, I started taking guitar lessons. This was a breakthrough in my creativity & courage, and not because I mastered the guitar by any means! I actually found it very difficult & initially frustrating, but I still managed to write several songs with a few chords. After work, I would meet with my guitar teacher in a small room in the back of a record store. The breakthrough in creativity came, because I let go of wanting to master the instrument. I only desired to have fun & explore! So much in the world is about mastering things, being a pro, & getting the "A" grade. I no longer put these demands on myself. Thank you, guitar!

ONE DAY I STARTED A NEW LIFE

When I was rebuilding my life, I bought a few small plants with each paycheck. Everything was new to me. I walked around saying kind words to the plants, touching their leaves. Some made it, some didn't. But over time I saw it appear, what I have today: my wild garden.

My Wild Garden, 14.5 x 11, watercolor pencils and pen on old book paper, 2020

When I was rebuilding my life, I bought a few small plants with each paycheck. Everything was new to me. I walked around saying kind words to the plants, touching their leaves. Some made it, some didn't. But over time I saw it appear, what I have today: my wild garden.

My Home in Santa Ana, 9.7 x 12.5, watercolor paint, watercolor pencils, plain paper, and pen on old book paper, 2020

I never imagined I would own a home. This didn't bother me, since I knew love & a happy life could be cultivated in the smallest apartment and I believed a house may be beyond my economic means. Still, in my early 40s a dream of getting my own peaceful home took hold of me. I kept a stack of beautiful books on houses and architecture next to my bed & believed they had special powers. At age 45, after wading through years of debt & other tough times, I bought my first home in Santa Ana, California. I lost my dad when I was 32 & my mom when I was 41, so they were never able to see this miracle, but someone told me that a house is a spiritual thing and this news reached them in heaven.

Above:
Books, 11 x 14.5, watercolor pencils, plain paper, magazine paper, recycled dictionary paper, and pen on old book paper, 2020

Thankful for…a heart of books – a soul of books - a life of books – a home of books

Opposite:
Memoir pages from my 7 x 9.7 sketchbook were created in 2020 using watercolor paint, watercolor pencils, pen, magazine paper, cardstock, and old book paper

Top: *Rena Gloria*

Tribute to my mom – Lifelong singer, connoisseur of everyday magic, resident of the Spirit World

Left: *Life of a Book Lover - Most Loved Books of My Life So Far*

Books featured: *All About Love* (bell hooks); *Teachings on Love* (Thich Nhat Hanh), *Communion* (bell hooks); *The Color Purple* (Alice Walker); *The Re-enchantment of Everyday Life* (Thomas Moore); *Women Who Run with the Wolves* (Clarissa Pinkola Estés); *The Little Locksmith* (Katharine Butler Hathaway); *Odes to Common Things* (Pablo Neruda); *An Unknown Woman* (Alice Koller); *Beloved* (Toni Morrison); *The Bridge of Beyond* (Simone Schwarz-Bart); *Their Eyes Were Watching God* (Zora Neale Hurston); *Through the Flower: My Struggle as a Woman Artist* (Judy Chicago); *On the Road* (Jack Kerouac); *Howl* (Allen Ginsberg); Mary Oliver's Poetry; *Common Woman Poems* (Judy Grahn); *Just Kids* (Patti Smith); *Goddesses in Everywoman* (Jean Shinoda Bolen); Poems & Essays of June Jordan; Emerson's Essays; and *Leaves of Grass* (Walt Whitman)

Right: *David Walter Shotsberger 1926-2002*

Tribute to my dad & his magnificent garden - Mechanicsburg, PA 1978

CHILDREN'S BOOK ILLUSTRATION

As I became more experimental and courageous with my artmaking, I started to make pieces that I call "collage illustrations," where I combine drawings with collage and mixed media techniques. In different contexts, when people saw my work, they asked if I was a children's book illustrator. This completely took me by surprise. At first, I just shrugged it off. Then this became an unexpected and enchanting part of my creative life.

One weekend I made a collage illustration where I imagined my dogs Joni and Walter as dog poets going to a poetry reading. Then I made a few more. This happened during the time when I just started my expressive arts certificate program. I was in a studio in Sarasota, Florida, for an intensive when another student saw a drawing I was making for a class assignment. "Do you illustrate children's books?" she asked me. There was a version of the question I had been hearing! I thought of the few images I had just made at home and responded, "I think I'm working on my first book!"

Working on the art for what would become the book *Poetry Hounds* (Litwin Books), my first children's book, was a beautiful time. I was immersed in the process, often laughing and dancing around while I drew my dogs Joni and Walter and cut out words and letters from magazines that I pasted above them. These words and letters were a way to represent their magic as dog poets. Sadly, Joni passed away after I completed all of the artwork, but before *Poetry Hounds* was published. I then saw the book as a tribute to her. Joni was a senior rescue dog from Coastal German Shepherd Rescue (as was Walter). Caring for Joni and witnessing her transformation during the almost five years we shared was one of the best experiences of my life. Named after Joni Mitchell, my beloved Joni howled her songs, both in the house and backyard, as she went from being a scared and neglected dog to a happy and well-loved dog. Joni's story of transformation shows that healing can take a long time, but we can heal at any age.

After *Poetry Hounds*, I began working on the collage illustrations for my second children's book: *Wild Librarian Bakery and Bookstore* (Litwin Books). It has been a dream of mine to open a community place that would be a combination bakery and bookstore. Since I do not have the financial means to do this, I have used my imagination to bring the place into existence through a children's book and the novel *Stella Peabody's Wild Librarian Bakery and Bookstore* (Wild Librarian Press).

Included in this section are images from *Poetry Hounds*, *Wild Librarian Bakery and Bookstore*, and unpublished works, including scenes from *Good Times in Dog City* and *Barry the Wolf*. I've included a few images from the zine *Joni, the Heavenly Dog Poet*, which was something I made to help mend my broken heart after Joni's passing. In the zine, I imagine Joni in Heaven, sending her poems down to Earth. I've also included some of my work in this section that seems to fit best within this category.

STACY RUSSO

Above:
Family Past and Present, 12.5 x 19, watercolor paint, acrylic paint, pen, and magazine paper on art paper, 2022

This work celebrates the magical beings, dogs and cats, I've been fortunate to have as family members over the past fifteen years.

Opposite:
Moon Watchers (Stacy and Walter), 22 x 17, watercolor paint, acrylic paint, pen, and magazine paper on mixed media paper, 2022

In late 2021, my dog Walter sustained a spontaneous and traumatic injury to his back, which resulted in him losing the use of his hind legs. I spent a difficult six months trying to help Walter rehabilitate following the injury and subsequent surgery. This involved taking him to therapy three times each week. Although it was a hard time, it was also one of the best experiences of my life that expanded my heart and made me more aware of what I am capable of. During this time, I used a harness to help Walter walk. We spent a lot of time in the front yard and garden, enjoying both the sun and the moon. I created this piece while caring for Walter and learning about the deep and powerful combined forces of love, commitment, and service. Walter passed away from an unrelated illness in May 2022. I will never know if he would have been able to regain his independence with walking, but we sure gave it everything we had during those months.

Moving Forward Together, 22 x 17, watercolor paint, watercolor pencils, pen, and magazine paper, 2022

Reading Magic, 24 x 18, watercolor paint, pen, and magazine paper on mixed media paper, 2020

ONE DAY I STARTED A NEW LIFE

Above:
Dog Poets in Heaven (Scene from Joni the Heavenly Dog Poet Zine), 11 x 14, watercolor paint, watercolor pencils, pen, and magazine paper on mixed media paper, 2020

Opposite:
Let's Go!, 12.5 x 19, watercolor paint, watercolor pencils, pen, and magazine paper on art paper, 2023

Let's Go! celebrates the adoption of my current dogs, Jack and Lily. Just like Joni and Walter, Jack and Lily are from Coastal German Shepherd Rescue.

Beautiful Community, 22.25 x 30, watercolor paint, pen, and magazine paper on art paper, 2020

Above:
Top: *Joni Over the Redwoods (Scene from Joni the Heavenly Dog Poet Zine)*, 11 x 14, watercolor paint, watercolor pencils, pen, and magazine paper on mixed media paper, 2020

Left: *Joni Sends Poems to the Food Gardens (Scene from Joni the Heavenly Dog Poet Zine)*, 11 x 14, watercolor paint, watercolor pencils, pen, and magazine paper on mixed media paper, 2020

Right: *Joni Sends Inspiration to Writers and Poets (Scene from Joni the Heavenly Dog Poet Zine)*, 11 x 14, watercolor paint, watercolor pencils, pen, and magazine paper on mixed media paper, 2020

Opposite:
Joni in Heaven (Scene from Joni the Heavenly Dog Poet Zine), 14 x 11, watercolor paint, watercolor pencils, pen, and magazine paper on mixed media paper, 2020

ONE DAY I STARTED A NEW LIFE

Above:
Barry Performs for His Community (Barry the Wolf Zine), 8.5 x 5.5, watercolor paint, acrylic paint, watercolor pencils, pen, and magazine paper on mixed media paper, 2021

Opposite:
Cover Art for Barry the Wolf Zine, 8.5 x 5.5, watercolor paint, acrylic paint, and pen on mixed media paper, 2021

Above:
Bow Wow Books and Cafe, 12.5 x 19, watercolor paint, pen, and magazine paper on mixed media paper, 2022

Opposite:
Flower Shop in Dog City (Scene from Good Times in Dog City), 11 x 14, watercolor paint, acrylic paint, watercolor pencils, pen, and magazine paper on mixed media paper, 2022

Following page spread:
Flying to Dog City (Scene from Good Times in Dog City), 11 x 14, watercolor paint, acrylic paint, watercolor pencils, pen, and magazine paper on mixed media paper, 2022

ONE DAY I STARTED A NEW LiFE

Above:
Full Moon Festival in Dog City (Scene from Good Times in Dog City), 11 x 14, watercolor paint, acrylic paint, watercolor pencils, pen, and magazine paper on mixed media paper, 2022

Opposite:
Shakespeare in the Park in Dog City (Scene from Good Times in Dog City), 11 x 14, watercolor paint, watercolor pencils, pen, and magazine paper on mixed media paper, 2022

Following page spread:
Stepping Out for the Night in Dog City (Scene from Good Times in Dog City), 11 x 14, watercolor paint, acrylic paint, watercolor pencils, pen, and magazine paper on mixed media paper, 2022

Typewriters (Scene from Poetry Hounds), 22 x 17, watercolor paint, pen, and magazine paper on art paper, 2020

Art Class (Scene from Poetry Hounds), 22 x 17, watercolor paint, pen, and magazine paper on art paper, 2020

Going to a Poetry Reading (Scene from Poetry Hounds), 22 x 17, watercolor paint, pen, lokta paper, and magazine paper on art paper, 2019

Above:
Meeting with Wise Old Tom (Scene from Poetry Hounds), 22 x 17, watercolor paint, pen, and magazine paper on art paper, 2020

Following page spread:
Yellow Home (Scene from Poetry Hounds), 17 x 22, watercolor paint, pen, and magazine paper on art paper, 2020

Stella Camping (Scene from Wild Librarian Bakery and Bookstore), 11 x 14, watercolor paint, acrylic paint, watercolor pencils, pen, and magazine paper on mixed media paper, 2021

Stella Reading Women Who Run with the Wolves (Scene from Wild Librarian Bakery and Bookstore), 11 x 14, watercolor paint, acrylic paint, watercolor pencils, pen, and magazine paper on mixed media paper, 2021

Poetry Reading (Scene from Wild Librarian Bakery and Bookstore), 14 x 11, watercolor paint, acrylic paint, watercolor pencils, pen, and magazine paper on mixed media paper, 2021

Stella Baking at Home (Scene from Wild Librarian Bakery and Bookstore), 11 x 14, watercolor paint, acrylic paint, watercolor pencils, pen, and magazine paper on mixed media paper, 2021

ONE DAY I STARTED A NEW LIFE

Above:
So Long Poetry Hounds—Until We Meet Again!, 18 x 24, watercolor paint, acrylic paint, pen, and magazine paper on mixed media paper, 2023

After the passing of my beloved dogs Joni and Walter, I imagined them as travelers in several works. This began with the one I titled *So Long Poetry Hounds—Until We Meet Again!*

Opposite:
Sometimes There is a Stirring in the Soul for Travel, 24 x 18, watercolor paint, pen, and magazine paper on mixed media paper, 2023

Following page spread:
Joni and Walter Writing Poems in San Francisco, 18 x 24, watercolor paint, pen, and magazine paper on mixed media paper, 2023

Opposite:
Joni and Walter in the Garden, 11 x 14, watercolor paint, acrylic paint, pen, and magazine paper on mixed media paper, 2021

Above:
Joy of Reading, 14 x 11, watercolor paint, watercolor pencils, pen, and magazine paper on mixed media paper, 2022

Joy of Reading is the cover art for the book *What Gets Them to Read Like That?*, the story of French librarian Geneviève Patte (Litwin Books, 2022).

Above:
Wilderness Gathering, 18 x 24, watercolor paint, watercolor pencils, pen, and magazine paper on mixed media paper, 2022

Opposite:
Some Families Look Different, 19 x 12.5, watercolor paint, pen, and magazine paper on art paper, 2023

ONE DAY I STARTED A NEW LIFE

Thank you for your interest in my work and discovering my creative journey. I believe we all have the power to create, bring joy into our lives, and heal our emotional and spiritual pain through artmaking. I hope that you discovered things on these pages that inspired you and connected with your life.

—**Stacy Russo, 2024**

www.ingramcontent.com/pod-product-compliance
Lightning Source LLC
Chambersburg PA
CBHW040907020526
44114CB00038B/84